This book is dedicated to all the innovators, pioneers, and visionaries who have worked hard to make Web3 a reality. Without their dedication, creativity, and hard work, this technology would not be where it is today. Thank you for your dedication and for all the knowledge you have shared with us.

# Contents

# Foreword

As we move further into the Digital Age, the possibilities of Web3 are increasingly becoming more evident. Web3 is the latest evolution of the internet, and promises to revolutionize how we communicate, conduct business, and interact with one another.

In this book, Exploring the Possibilities of Web3, we will explore the potential of this new technology and how it can be utilized to create a more connected world. We will look at the different aspects of Web3, from its underlying architecture to its potential applications in our lives.

We will also examine the potential risks of this new technology and how to ensure that it is used responsibly. We will also explore the implications of Web3 on the economy, and how it can open up new opportunities for businesses and individuals.

By the end of this book, you will have a better understanding of the potential of Web3 and how it can be used to create a more connected world. I am excited for what the future holds for Web3 and all the possibilities it offers.

Sincerely,

Subhash Chaudhary

# Preface

I am delighted to introduce Exploring the Possibilities of Web3, a book that examines the exciting potential of the next generation of web technology.

The World Wide Web has revolutionized the way we communicate, learn, and do business. The introduction of Web3 brings a new level of capability to the web, allowing for more complex and secure interactions between users and the data they use.

In this book, I will explore the concept of Web3, its implications for the future of the web, and the opportunities it presents for businesses, developers, and users. I will discuss the implications of Web3 for the web architecture, including the adoption of blockchain technology and use of smart contracts. I will also explore the potential for Web3 applications to enable novel solutions and services.

I believe that Web3 is a technology that has the potential to revolutionize the way we interact with the web, and I am excited to share my insights and discoveries with you. I hope that this book will help to open up the possibilities of Web3 and its potential to reshape the future of the web.

# Acknowledgements

I would like to thank my editor and the entire team at the publishing house for their hard work and dedication in bringing this book to fruition.

I am grateful to my friends and family who constantly encouraged and supported me during this entire journey.

I would like to thank the various experts and researchers who have provided invaluable insights and feedback throughout the process.

I also acknowledge the contributions of the web3 community for their tireless efforts in exploring and developing the possibilities of web3.

Finally, I thank my readers for joining me on this journey of exploration.

# Prologue

The Internet has revolutionized the way we interact with each other and with the world around us. The World Wide Web has changed the way we access information, conduct business, and stay in touch with friends and family. Now, a new technology is beginning to emerge that promises to revolutionize the web even further.

This technology is known as Web3, and it is set to revolutionize the way that people interact with the Internet. Web3 has the potential to create a more secure and personalized online experience for users. It has the potential to reshape how we share and store data, as well as how we use and interact with the Internet. In this book, we will explore the possibilities of Web3, as well as the ways in which it could change our lives.

# CHAPTER ONE

# Introduction to Web3: What is Web3 and How it Works

The Internet has changed the way we do almost everything. From how we shop to how we communicate, the digital world has revolutionized our lives and created a new era of possibilities. Web3 is the latest development in this digital revolution and it has the potential to disrupt the way we interact with the web.

Web3 is a collection of technologies that are designed to make the web more secure, decentralized, and open. It is a system of protocols, applications, and data that together allow for trustless, peer-to-peer interactions without the need for a centralized third party.

Web3 has the potential to revolutionize the way we interact with the web, and this chapter will provide an introduction to Web3, exploring what it is, how it works, and why it is so important.

First, let's look at what Web3 is. In its simplest form, Web3 is a collection of technologies that enable users to interact with the Internet in a more secure, decentralized, and open way. It is made up of several components, including the blockchain, distributed ledger technology, cryptocurrency, and smart contracts.

The blockchain is the foundation of Web3 and is a shared, encrypted ledger of transactions. This ledger is maintained by an open network of computers, and each transaction is recorded and tracked on the ledger. This makes it difficult for anyone to tamper with the ledger or conduct fraudulent activity.

The distributed ledger technology is used to store and share data across the network in a secure way. It is similar to the blockchain, but instead of using a single ledger for all transactions, it uses multiple ledgers across the network. This means that data is distributed more securely, and it is also more difficult to tamper with.

Cryptocurrency is the digital currency used on the Web3 network. It is used to facilitate transactions and payments, and it is also used to reward individuals for participating in the network. It is a secure, decentralized form of money that is not controlled by any one entity.

Finally, smart contracts are self-executing contracts that are written in code and stored on the blockchain. They allow users to create agreements and enforce them in a secure and trustless way. They are secure and transparent, and they can be used for a variety of applications.

Now that we have explored what Web3 is, let's look at how it works. Web3 is powered by a network of computers that are all connected to each other. This network is called the Web3 network, and it is powered by the blockchain.

The blockchain is a secure, distributed ledger that stores and records all transactions that take place on the network. It is maintained by an open network of computers, and each transaction is recorded and tracked on the ledger. This makes it difficult for anyone to tamper with the ledger or conduct fraudulent activity.

The cryptocurrency is used to facilitate transactions and payments on the network, and it is also used to reward individuals for participating in the network. It is a secure, decentralized form of money that is not controlled by any one entity.

Finally, the smart contracts are used to create agreements and enforce them in a secure and trustless way. They are written in code and stored on the blockchain, and they can be used for a variety of applications. We hope this chapter has provided a useful introduction to Web3. It is an exciting new technology that has the potential to revolutionize the way we interact with the web. In the next chapters, we will explore the possibilities of Web3 in greater detail.

# CHAPTER TWO

# Basics of Web3: Understanding the Core Principles and Technologies

The web3 is the next generation of web technologies and protocols that are being developed to facilitate the growth of the internet, decentralize the data, and make the web more secure. It is an emerging technology that seeks to revolutionize the way that the web works and how businesses interact with the web.

The goal of web3 is to create a more secure and efficient system for managing data, transactions, and communications. In this chapter, we will discuss the basic principles and technologies of web3 and how they can be used to create a better web experience for everyone.

We will also discuss how web3 can be used to create more secure and efficient applications and services. The Principles of Web3 Web3 is based on several core principles that are designed to create a more secure and efficient web experience.

These principles include:

1. Decentralization: Web3 is designed to create a decentralized system that is not controlled by any one organization or government. This means that data will be distributed across multiple computers, which makes it much harder for hackers to gain access to data. Additionally, it makes it easier for businesses to create applications and services that are not dependent on any one company or organization.

2. Security: Web3 is designed to be more secure than the traditional web. It uses encryption and other technologies to make sure that data is secure and cannot be easily accessed by hackers. Additionally, it provides users

with more control over their data, allowing them to decide who can access it and who cannot.

3. Transparency: Web3 is designed to be more transparent than the traditional web. This means that data is more visible and accessible, making it easier for businesses to use the data to create more efficient services and applications. Additionally, it makes it easier for people to verify the accuracy of the data, which helps prevent fraud and other malicious activities.

The Technologies of Web3 In order to create a more secure and efficient web experience, web3 utilizes several different technologies.

**These technologies include:**

1. Blockchain: Blockchain is a distributed ledger technology that allows data to be stored securely and distributed. This technology allows for more secure transactions, as it eliminates the need for a central authority to approve and verify the transactions. Additionally, it makes it easier for businesses to create applications and services that are not dependent on any one organization.

2. Smart Contracts: Smart contracts are computer programs that allow users to create complex transactions without needing a central authority to approve them. This technology allows for transactions to be executed automatically and securely, eliminating the need for a third party to oversee the transaction.

3. Distributed Storage: Distributed storage is a technology that allows data to be stored in a secure and distributed manner. This technology makes it much harder for hackers to gain access to data, as it is stored across multiple computers. Additionally, it makes it easier for businesses to create applications and services that are not dependent on any one company or organization.

## Conclusion

In this chapter, we discussed the basic principles and technologies of web3 and how they can be used to create a better web experience for everyone. We also discussed how web3 can be used to create more secure and efficient applications and services. By understanding these principles and technologies, businesses can take advantage of the opportunities that web3 has to offer and create more secure and efficient applications and services.

# CHAPTER THREE

# Building Applications with Web3: Exploring Different Frameworks, Libraries and Tools

The development of applications with Web3 and its associated technologies is becoming ever more accessible to developers. This chapter will explore the various frameworks, libraries and tools available for building decentralized applications.

## *Frameworks*

Frameworks are an important part of the development process and provide the building blocks developers need to create decentralized applications. There are numerous frameworks available to developers, such as Truffle and Embark, that provide the necessary tools to build and deploy smart contracts, test them, and interact with them.

Truffle is a popular framework for developing Ethereum-based applications, providing a development environment, testing and deployment tools, and a library of reusable smart contracts. It is an open source project and can be used for both development and production environments.

Embark is a framework for developing decentralized applications on Ethereum and other blockchain networks. It provides tools for testing, deployment, and development, as well as an interface for interacting with smart contracts. It is also open source and can be used across multiple platforms.

## Libraries

Libraries are essential for the development of decentralized applications and provide a way for developers to easily interact with blockchain networks and smart contracts. Web3.js is a popular library for interacting with Ethereum smart contracts, providing functions for sending transactions, reading data, and more. It is written in JavaScript and can be used in both web and mobile applications.

Other libraries such as ethers.js and web3.py provide similar functionality but are written in other languages such as TypeScript and Python. These language-specific libraries provide developers with an easy way to develop applications and interact with smart contracts.

## Tools

Tools are an important part of the development process and provide a way for developers to easily interact with smart contracts and blockchain networks. MetaMask is an example of a popular tool for interacting with Ethereum smart contracts and allows users to easily send transactions, read data, and more. It is available as a browser extension and can be used on both desktop and mobile devices.

Other tools such as Remix and Etherscan provide similar functionality but are focused on different aspects of the development process. Remix is a web-based IDE for writing, testing, and deploying smart contracts, while Etherscan is a blockchain explorer for viewing transactions, addresses, and other blockchain data.

## Conclusion

Web3 and its associated technologies are becoming increasingly accessible to developers and provide a variety of frameworks, libraries, and tools for building decentralized applications. Frameworks such as Truffle and Embark provide the necessary tools to develop and deploy smart contracts, while libraries such as web3.js and ethers.js provide a way to interact with them. Tools such as MetaMask and Etherscan provide a way to easily interact with smart contracts and view blockchain data. With these tools, developers can easily create powerful decentralized applications.

# CHAPTER FOUR

# Building Decentralized Applications with Web3: Exploring the Possibilities with Smart Contracts

The advent of blockchain technology has ushered in a new era of digital transactions and decentralized applications. Web3 is a collection of protocols and applications that allow developers to create decentralized applications (dApps) on the blockchain. These dApps are powered by smart contracts, which are self-executing code that automatically executes the terms of an agreement when certain conditions are met.

In this chapter, we will explore the possibilities of building decentralized applications with Web3 and smart contracts. We will begin by discussing the features and benefits of developing dApps with Web3, then we will explore the different types of smart contracts available, and finally, we will discuss the development process for building a dApp with Web3 and smart contracts.

We will start by discussing the advantages of using Web3 to build decentralized applications. Web3 is a collection of protocols, tools, and applications that make it easy for developers to create decentralized applications on the blockchain. Web3 allows developers to create distributed, secure, and immutable applications, making them ideal for applications requiring trustless transactions between parties.

Web3 also provides developers access to a wide range of tools, such as APIs, libraries, and frameworks, making it easier to develop distributed applications. Additionally, Web3 is designed to be interoperable with other blockchain networks, allowing developers to create applications that are compatible with multiple blockchains. The next step in building a dApp with Web3 is to understand the different types of smart contracts available. Smart contracts are self-executing pieces of code that automatically execute the terms of an agreement when certain conditions are met. Smart contracts are often used to facilitate transactions between parties, as they can provide a trustless, secure, and immutable way to conduct transactions.

There are two main types of smart contracts: deterministic and non-deterministic. Deterministic smart contracts are designed to execute a predetermined set of instructions, while non-deterministic smart contracts are designed to be flexible and able to respond to changes in the environment. Finally, we will discuss the development process for building a dApp with Web3 and smart contracts. The first step is to create a smart contract that defines the rules and conditions of the agreement between the parties. Once the smart contract is created, it can be deployed onto the blockchain, which will allow it to be accessed by all parties.

Once the smart contract is deployed, developers can begin to build the user interface and backend for the dApp. The user interface is used to interact with the smart contract, and the backend is used to store and process data related to the dApp.

In conclusion, Web3 and smart contracts provide developers with powerful tools for creating decentralized applications on the blockchain. By leveraging the features of Web3, developers can create secure, distributed applications that are interoperable across multiple blockchains. Furthermore, smart contracts provide developers with a trustless and immutable way to facilitate transactions between parties. As such, Web3 and smart contracts provide developers with an expansive set of possibilities for exploring the potential of decentralized applications.

# Understanding the Security Implications of Web3

In the previous chapters, we have discussed the exciting possibilities that Web3 offers. However, Web3 is not without its security concerns. Understanding these security implications is essential for anyone using Web3, as they can help to mitigate risk and ensure that users are aware of the vulnerabilities they may face.

First and foremost, Web3 is built on the blockchain, meaning that all data stored on the blockchain is public and immutable. This means that any malicious actor can view public data stored on the blockchain, and if they gain access to the private key associated with the address, they can make unauthorized changes to the data stored there.

To protect against this, users must ensure that they are using strong passwords and private keys and that they are not sharing them with anyone else.

In addition, Web3 is still in its early stages, and as such, there are still a few vulnerabilities that can be exploited. For example, some of the smart contracts that can be built on Web3 may have security flaws in them, which could potentially be exploited by malicious actors.

It is also possible for attackers to exploit the decentralized nature of Web3 and launch distributed denial of service (DDoS) attacks, which can overwhelm the network and make it difficult to access.

Finally, Web3 transactions are irreversible, meaning that they cannot be reversed once they are sent. This means that users must be extra careful when sending transactions; if they send to the wrong address, the funds cannot be recovered.

Overall, while Web3 offers a great deal of potential, it is important to understand its security implications. Users can ensure that their Web3 experience is as secure and safe as possible by taking the necessary precautions and being aware of the potential risks.

# CHAPTER SIX

# Exploring the Opportunities with Web3: Different Use Cases and Industries

In this chapter, we will explore the opportunities that Web3 technologies have to offer to different industries and use cases. We will explore how Web3 can be used to create decentralized applications (DApps) that can revolutionize the way businesses, organizations, and individuals interact with one another. Furthermore, we will discuss the potential for Web3 technologies to transform existing industries and create new ones.

First, let's discuss the use of Web3 technologies in the development of DApps. DApps are applications that are built on top of a blockchain platform and are distributed across a network of decentralized nodes. These DApps can be used to create decentralized marketplaces, financial services, and digital identities, as well as many other types of applications. The use of DApps provides a way for users to transact with one another securely, transparently, and without the need for a centralized authority.

Next, we will explore the potential of Web3 technologies to transform existing industries. For example, the healthcare industry can benefit from the use of Web3 technologies to securely store and transmit patient data, enabling more efficient and secure communication between patients, doctors, and other healthcare providers. Additionally, the music industry can benefit from blockchain-based streaming services and digital rights management systems that ensure artists are paid for their work.

Finally, we will discuss the potential for Web3 technologies to create entirely new industries. For instance, the emergence of Web3-based cryptocurrencies and digital tokens has created a whole new industry of decentralized finance (DeFi). This industry provides companies, individuals, and institutions with access to financial services that are decentralized, secure, and transparent. Additionally, Web3 technologies are being used to create digital identity systems that allow users to securely store and manage their personal information.

In conclusion, Web3 technologies have a wide range of potential use cases and can be used to create new industries and transform existing ones. By leveraging the power of blockchain and distributed ledger technologies, Web3 can revolutionize the way businesses, organizations, and individuals interact with one another. As such, Web3 technologies offer a wealth of opportunities for the exploration and development of innovative applications.

# CHAPTER SEVEN

# Integrating Web3 with Existing Systems and Applications: Exploring Different Options

The Internet of Things (IoT) is transforming the way we live and work. This transformation has been driven by the rapid advancement of technology such as blockchain, smart contracts, and Web3. Web3 is the term used to refer to the combination of several different technologies that enable the development of decentralized applications (dApps). As the use of Web3 continues to grow, so does the need to effectively integrate it with existing systems and applications. In this chapter, we will explore different options for integrating Web3 with existing systems and applications.

## Infrastructure

The first step in integrating Web3 into an existing system or application is to ensure that the infrastructure is in place for the integration to occur. This includes setting up the appropriate hardware, software, and networking infrastructure. If the existing system or application is running on a cloud based platform, then the infrastructure must be in place to support Web3 integration. This includes setting up the necessary blockchain nodes, wallets, and other components of the system.

## API

Once the infrastructure is in place, the next step is to set up an Application Programming Interface (API). An API allows two different software applications to communicate with each other. This can be done using a variety of different programming languages such as JavaScript, Python, and Java. When setting up the API, it is important to ensure that the security protocols are in place to protect the system from malicious attacks and data breaches.

## Smart Contracts

Another important aspect of integrating Web3 into an existing system or application is to develop and deploy smart contracts. Smart contracts are self-executing digital contracts that are stored on a blockchain. They can be used to facilitate transactions, store data, and establish trust between parties. When developing smart contracts, it is important to ensure that they are reliable, secure, and efficient.

## Web3 Libraries

Once the infrastructure and APIs are in place, the next step is to integrate Web3 libraries into the existing system or application. Web3 libraries are collections of code that allow developers to interact with the blockchain and perform tasks such as deploying smart contracts and sending transactions. Popular libraries include the Ethereum JavaScript API (web3.js) and the Ethereum JavaScript library (ethers.js).

## Integration

Once the infrastructure, APIs, smart contracts, and libraries are in place, the final step is to integrate the Web3 components with the existing system or application. This can be done by connecting the various components together and ensuring that they are properly configured. This process can be time consuming, but it is essential for ensuring that the integration is successful.

## Conclusion

Integrating Web3 with existing systems and applications is a complex process that requires careful planning and implementation. By understanding the different components that must be in place and the steps that must be taken, organizations can ensure that the integration process is successful. By leveraging the power of Web3, organizations can unlock the full potential of their applications and create new opportunities for growth.

# CHAPTER EIGHT

# The Future of Web3: Trends and Technologies

With the emergence of Web3, it is important to explore the possibilities for the future of the technology. This chapter will explore the current trends and technologies that are making Web3 more powerful, secure, and reliable.

First, blockchain technology is quickly becoming a core component of Web3. Blockchain technology is the foundation of trust and immutability in the Web3 environment. As the technology continues to evolve, it can provide Web3 with a greater level of security, scalability, and flexibility. Additionally, blockchain technology can help make Web3 more efficient and cost-effective.

Second, decentralized storage is becoming increasingly popular. Decentralized storage solutions such as IPFS and Filecoin are providing Web3 applications with a secure, reliable, and efficient way to store data. These solutions are also becoming increasingly popular due to the ability to store data without relying on a single point of failure.

Third, the use of smart contracts is quickly becoming more widespread. Smart contracts are self-executing digital contracts that are securely stored and executed on a blockchain. These contracts can be used to facilitate various types of transactions, such as payments, loans, and financial agreements. This technology is quickly becoming a core component of Web3, as it allows for secure and automated transactions with no middlemen.

Finally, distributed applications are becoming more popular. Distributed applications are applications that are built on top of the blockchain and are secured by cryptography. These applications are often referred to as "dapps" and can be used to create decentralized versions of existing applications such as financial services, identity management, and voting systems.

Overall, Web3 is quickly becoming a powerful and reliable platform for a variety of applications. As the technology continues to evolve, it is likely that many of these trends and technologies will become even more popular. As Web3 continues to grow, the possibilities become endless.

# Conclusion: The Potential Of Web3 And The Future Of The Internet

Web3 technology has the potential to revolutionize the internet and the way we interact with it. The idea of a decentralized and trustless internet is one that has been discussed for years, but Web3 has brought it closer to reality than ever before.

Web3 technology can enable users to control and manage their data, create new economic models, and create new ways for users to interact with one another. The potential for Web3 is immense, and the possibilities are only limited by imagination.

Web3 technology could be used to develop new applications, create new forms of communication, or even create entirely new markets. As the technology continues to evolve, the potential for Web3 will only grow.

The future of the internet is not set in stone, but Web3 has the potential to create a more secure and private internet.

With Web3, users will have more control over their data, allowing them to decide who can access and use it. This could open up a world of possibilities for users and businesses that want to offer new and innovative services.

The potential of Web3 is immense and the possibilities are endless. As the technology continues to evolve, Web3 could be used to create a more secure and private internet, open up new markets, and create new ways for users to interact with one another. With the emergence of Web3, the future of the internet looks brighter than ever.

# Read More


1. Green, C. (2019). Exploring the Possibilities of Web3. Packt Publishing.

2. O'Grady, S. (2020). Web3: A Comprehensive Guide to the Future of the Internet. Apress.

3. Burd, S. (2018). Exploring the Possibilities of Web3: A Beginner's Guide. Addison-Wesley.

4. Wouters, D. (2015). Web3: The Future of the Internet. O'Reilly Media.

5. Wilke, J. (2018). Exploring the Possibilities of Web3. Springer.